Buffa

THE SCHOMBURG CENTER FOR RESEARCH IN BLACK CULTURE

THE NEW YORK PUBLIC LIBRARY

Pomegranate

SAN FRANCISCO

Pomegranate Communications, Inc.
Box 808022, Petaluma, California 94975
800-227-1428 ■ www.pomegranate.com

Pomegranate Europe Ltd.
Unit 1, Heathcote Business Centre, Hurlbutt Road
Warwick, Warwickshire CV34 6TD, U.K. ■ [+44] 0 1926 430111

ISBN 0-7649-2878-3
Pomegranate Catalog No. AA242

Pomegranate publishes books of postcards on a wide range of subjects.
Please contact the publisher for more information.

Cover designed by Patrice Morris
Printed in China

13 12 11 10 09 08 07 06 05 04   10 9 8 7 6 5 4 3 2 1

To facilitate detachment of the postcards from this book, fold each card along its perforation line before tearing.

The first black people I ever saw in a TV western were Ivan Dixon and folksinger Odetta, in an episode of *Have Gun Will Travel*. I was shocked. I thought: "Geez. There might've been a couple of black people in the West."

Even though the Buffalo Soldiers comprised 20 percent of the army of the Plains, I never heard of them as a youngster; never read about them; never saw them on TV or in the movies. That really bothered me—but that was how the history of our country had always been presented to me.

I found out later that the Buffalo Soldiers were significantly involved in historic military events, from the Plains Indian Wars through World War I. Throughout the Southwest desert and in the central and northern Plains, they fought bands of Native Americans, including renegade bands led by legendary warriors like Victorio and Geronimo.

Their duty was the toughest the army could offer, in the most remote, uninhabitable terrain, and under primitive conditions. The life was lonely and demanding. They slept on bug-infested, wooden bunks in dusty barracks with no bathtubs. Colds, pneumonia, and other infectious diseases cost more soldiers their lives than shootouts with Indians. Between 1870 and 1890, the Ninth and Tenth Cavalries fought sixty battles, including dozens against Geronimo and Victorio. They earned at least eighteen Medals of Honor, eleven of which were awarded to members of the Ninth. Their protection of settlers was legendary. While blacks on the Plains risked their lives every day in defense of others, racism and injustice dogged their heels.

Buffalo Soldiers were sent to the Plains to accomplish more than the army had ever asked of any military unit in the field: help build roads and lay railroad track; string telegraph wire; capture cattle rustlers and horse thieves; guard the southern border; protect migrating white settlers; maintain peace among the settlers, cattlemen, Indians defending their home-land, ruthless outlaws, and raiding Mexican bandits.

Their enormous contribution has not been forgotten. It is reflected in their stories, and in the twenty-eight images presented here of honorable, brave, and hardy soldiers whose indomitable spirit shaped America.

—Kareem Abdul-Jabbar

Buffalo Soldiers

Captain Charles Young
West Point, New York, 1889
Collection of Anthony L. Powell
© Anthony L. Powell

BOX 808022   PETALUMA   CA 94975

Pomegranate

Buffalo Soldiers

President William H. Taft with black 1st sergeant, 1911
Collection of Anthony L. Powell
© Anthony L. Powell

BOX 808022 PETALUMA CA 94975

Pomegranate

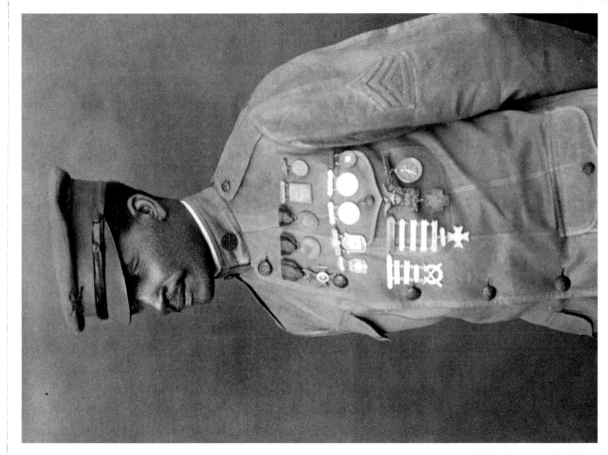

Buffalo Soldiers

Sergeant Tate, best rifle shot in the Army, Twenty-fifth Infantry
Fort Lawton, Washington, 1909
Collection of Anthony L. Powell
© Anthony L. Powell

BOX 808022   PETALUMA   CA 94975

Pomegranate

TROOP E, NINTH CAVALRY

Buffalo Soldiers

Troop E, Ninth Cavalry, 1909
Collection of Anthony L. Powell
© Anthony L. Powell

BOX 808022 PETALUMA CA 94975

Pomegranate

Buffalo Soldiers

Regimental Commissary Sergeant Buck
Fort Lawton, Washington, 1909
Collection of Anthony L. Powell
© Anthony L. Powell

BOX 808022   PETALUMA   CA 94975

Pomegranate

Buffalo Soldiers

Four black chaplains in the U.S. Army: Scout, Gladden,
Anderson, and Prioleau

Madison Barracks, New York, 1908

Collection of Anthony L. Powell

© Anthony L. Powell

BOX 808022   PETALUMA   CA 94975

Pomegranate

Buffalo Soldiers

Troopers of the Tenth Cavalry
Montana, 1906
Collection of Anthony L. Powell
© Anthony L. Powell

BOX 808022   PETALUMA   CA 94975

Pomegranate

Buffalo Soldiers

Sergeant Major Spotswood W. Taliaferro and his wife
Fort Lawton, Washington, 1910
Collection of Anthony L. Powell
© Anthony L. Powell

BOX 808022   PETALUMA   CA 94975

Pomegranate

Buffalo Soldiers

Soldier, Twenty-fifth Infantry
Fort Lawton, Washington, 1909
Collection of Anthony L. Powell
© Anthony L. Powell

BOX 808022   PETALUMA   CA 94975

Pomegranate

Buffalo Soldiers

Christmas Day
Fort Robinson, Nebraska, 1890
Collection of Anthony L. Powell
© Anthony L. Powell

BOX 808022   PETALUMA   CA 94975

Pomegranate

Buffalo Soldiers

Officers of the Twenty-fifth Infantry, 1901

Collection of Anthony L. Powell

© Anthony L. Powell

BOX 808022   PETALUMA   CA 94975

Pomegranate

Buffalo Soldiers

Noncommissioned staff of the Tenth Cavalry
Fort Robinson, Nebraska, 1906
Collection of Anthony L. Powell
© Anthony L. Powell

BOX 808022   PETALUMA   CA 94975

Pomegranate

Buffalo Soldiers

"Life Was Good in Those Days."
Band members and families, Twenty-fifth Infantry
Fort Lawton, Washington, 1910
Collection of Anthony L. Powell
© Anthony L. Powell

BOX 808022   PETALUMA   CA 94975

Pomegranate

Buffalo Soldiers

Noncommissioned officers of Troop H, 1909
Collection of Anthony L. Powell
© Anthony L. Powell

BOX 808022   PETALUMA   CA 94975

Pomegranate

Buffalo Soldiers

Chaplain George W. Prioleau and family, Ninth Cavalry
San Francisco, 1904
Collection of Anthony L. Powell
© Anthony L. Powell

BOX 808022 PETALUMA CA 94975

Pomegranate

Buffalo Soldiers

Two soldiers of the Tenth Cavalry
Arizona, 1913
Collection of Anthony L. Powell
© Anthony L. Powell

BOX 808022   PETALUMA   CA 94975

Pomegranate

Buffalo Soldiers

Noncommissioned staff, Twenty-fourth Infantry
Madison Barracks, New York, 1909
Collection of Anthony L. Powell
© Anthony L. Powell

BOX 808022   PETALUMA   CA 94975

Pomegranate

Buffalo Soldiers

Home of bandleader Leslie King
Fort Huachuca, Arizona, c. 1900
Collection of Anthony L. Powell
© Anthony L. Powell

BOX 808022   PETALUMA   CA 94975

Pomegranate

Buffalo Soldiers

Trooper sounding retreat, Ninth Cavalry
Fort Keough, Montana, 1890
Collection of Anthony L. Powell
© Anthony L. Powell

BOX 808022   PETALUMA   CA 94975

Pomegranate

Colored troops at Ft. Grant Ariz

Buffalo Soldiers

Colored troops
Fort Grant, Arizona, 1898
Collection of Kareem Abdul-Jabbar
© Kareem Abdul-Jabbar

BOX 808022   PETALUMA   CA 94975

Pomegranate

Glass, chief of scouts, Ft Apache, Ariz. 20.

Buffalo Soldiers

John T. Glass, scout, c. 1885

Collection of Kareem Abdul-Jabbar

© Kareem Abdul-Jabbar

BOX 808022 PETALUMA CA 94975

Pomegranate

Buffalo Soldiers

Tenth Cavalry
Fort Stockton, Texas, c. 1890
Collection of Kareem Abdul-Jabbar
© Kareem Abdul-Jabbar

BOX 808022   PETALUMA   CA 94975

Pomegranate

Buffalo Soldiers

Rifle team, c. 1885
Collection of Kareem Abdul-Jabbar
© Kareem Abdul-Jabbar

BOX 808022   PETALUMA   CA 94975

Pomegranate

COMPANY H 24 U.S. INF. PHILIPPINE ISLANDS.

Buffalo Soldiers

Company H, Twenty-fourth Infantry
Philippine Islands, c. 1900
Collection of Kareem Abdul-Jabbar
© Kareem Abdul-Jabbar

BOX 808022   PETALUMA   CA 94975

Pomegranate

Buffalo Soldiers

Members of the Twenty-fourth Infantry Band
Fort Douglas, Utah, 1899
Collection of Anthony L. Powell
© Anthony L. Powell

BOX 808022   PETALUMA   CA 94975

Pomegranate

Buffalo Soldiers

Baseball team of Company B, Twenty-fourth Infantry
Madison Barracks, New York, 1908
Collection of Anthony L. Powell
© Anthony L. Powell

BOX 808022   PETALUMA   CA 94975

Pomegranate

HARPER'S WEEKLY.

A JOURNAL OF CIVILIZATION.

Vol. XXX.—No. 1548.

NEW YORK, SATURDAY, AUGUST 21, 1886.

Copyright, 1886, by Harper & Brothers.

TEN CENTS A COPY.
WITH A SUPPLEMENT.

Buffalo Soldiers

Lt. Powhatan H. Clarke, Tenth Cavalry
Artist: Frederick Remington
Harper's Weekly, August 21, 1886
Collection of Kareem Abdul-Jabbar
© Kareem Abdul-Jabbar

BOX 808022   PETALUMA   CA 94975

Pomegranate

Buffalo Soldiers

Privates James Satchell and Samuel Tipton
Ninth Cavalry, Troop C, 1891
Collection of Anthony L. Powell
© Anthony L. Powell

BOX 808022   PETALUMA   CA 94975

Pomegranate